50 Odd Couples

the dodo

50 Odd Couples

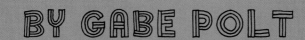

the dodo

BY GABE POLT

Scholastic Inc.

TABLE OF CONTENTS

INTRODUCTION

Friends come in all shapes and sizes—and that's especially true for these fifty unlikely animal pairs! From giant horses to tiny squirrels, and fluffy ducks to fuzzy pigs, the animals in this book know that sometimes you can find a best friend in the most unexpected ways. After all, it doesn't matter what your friends look like. The most important part of any friendship is having fun together!

These animal odd couples show their love for their friends in all sorts of ways. You'll meet a cat who takes care of a baby squirrel, a dog who gets a ride from his donkey best friend, a goat who tucks in a baby bull at bedtime, and many more adorable true stories.

Whether these animals are covered in fur or feathers, walk on two webbed feet or four strong hooves, or say hello with a bleat or a meow, they all have one important thing in common: They're happy to show their love to their friends. So turn the page and get ready for lots of cuddles, lots of mischief, and lots of awesome animal friendships!

BLOSSOM AND MINNOW

Just like most siblings, Blossom and Minnow spend their days having fun and getting into trouble. They take turns stealing each other's toys, they enjoy playing dress-up, and after a full day, they like to snuggle together on the couch.

When this shaggy dog and snow-white turkey first met, no one planned for them to become forever friends. Blossom was rescued from a factory. She was supposed to stay at an animal shelter, but the shelter made her nervous and confused.

A shelter worker named Abbie had an idea. She thought staying with a family might help keep Blossom calm. Abbie's plan was to foster Blossom for a little while and then send her to a proper turkey sanctuary. But Blossom and Abbie's dog,

Minnow, had other plans.

As soon as Blossom waddled through the front door of Abbie's house, she headed straight to Minnow's dog bed, plopped down, and relaxed. As far as Blossom was concerned, she was home. Minnow agreed.

Soon the dog and turkey were just like siblings. Minnow has taught Blossom all about life in her new neighborhood. Minnow has a special ability to calm Blossom when she is agitated by an unexpected noise. Blossom takes good care of Minnow in return. She uses her beak to groom and preen Minnow's fur.

Whether Minnow and Blossom are taking a snooze in their side-by-side beds, sneaking bites of Abbie's burrito, or hiking through the Virginia countryside, this odd couple is happiest when they're together.

Morris spent the first nine months of his life in an animal shelter. Living in a shelter can be hard. Animals often spend most of their time alone in a small cage, so it's difficult to make friends.

But today, Morris's life is so different. The 15-pound cat spends his days exploring a sprawling farm with his best friend: a 900-pound chestnut horse named Champy!

This unusual friendship began when a woman named Jennifer adopted Morris when he was just a scared black kitten. Jennifer slowly introduced him to life on her farm. When Morris had his first trip outside, the cat was curious about his new neighbors. But someone else was even more curious—Champy!

Casino, New South Wales, Australia

CHAMPY AND MORRIS

Morris wears rain gear so he never misses a day of riding.

Every day Champy wandered over to nuzzle Morris, as if he were saying, "Won't you be my friend?" Before too long, Morris finally showed some interest in the big horse—by hopping up on Champy's back! The next thing Jennifer knew, the two of them were strolling around the yard.

Champy had never let anyone—human or animal—ride him before Morris.

Now Champy and Morris spend every day together. They usually start with a walk around the yard, with Morris perched on top of Champy's back. After a bit, they might take a break for a drink from the horses' massive water trough. Then the two friends will end the day by grooming each other. Champy is careful to be extra gentle as he licks his tiny cat friend. And then, when it's Morris's turn, the cat helps Champy keep his long mane clean. What a friend!

BANDITO

AND LUIGI

📍 Marbella, Spain

Bandito and Luigi's caretaker Finn says this odd couple is inseparable! "They eat, sleep, fight, snore, dart, and chase each other around constantly—every day!"

Bandito looks like most pugs. He has a short, tan coat; a black face mask; and an adorably wrinkly brow. From the rear, Bandito looks like a pig, thanks to his curly tail. His best friend in the world is Luigi, a serious-looking cat with soft gray,

The first pugs lived some 2,000 years ago in China.

black, and white stripes and copper eyes. His unique ears are a sign that Luigi is a breed called a Scottish Fold. In 2016, Bandito and Luigi made history by being the first dog and cat pair to hike the 497-mile-long Camino de Santiago, a trail that ends in Galicia, Spain. For six weeks these playmates lived on the road. They slept in tents and hiked with Finn and their other caretaker Sebastian across sunny Spain. Well, Bandito and Luigi did *some* walking. Other times they traveled by dog wagon and hitched *lots* of rides perched on their humans' backpacks!

Off the trail, Bandito and Luigi spend hours licking and nuzzling each other. First, Bandito creeps over to Luigi and licks his brow, then his nose, then his chin. Eventually, Luigi returns the licks and everyone gets a good "clean" cuddle. According to Finn, the two furry friends fill their days by getting into trouble. But once it gets close to dinnertime, they turn extra sweet, hoping for some watermelon—the brothers' favorite treat!

Scottish Fold kittens are born with straight ears, but they fold after about three weeks.

THE PACK: GERDY, JAKE, ROSE, AND DONALD

📍 St. Louis, Missouri

There is something very special about Kasey and Blake's family photos. Their pack includes not only humans, but a cat, dogs, and ducks, too!

But out of everyone in this blended family, the two American pit bull terriers, Rose and Jake, and two of the domestic ducks, Gerdy and Donald, have an extra special bond. The pitties were each rescued from unhappy and unsafe situations. Rose is the red-orange pit bull terrier, famous in her pack for being a Frisbee superstar who can jump six feet in the air. Jake is gray and a loyal companion to everyone in his family. He's always up for learning new tricks!

Gerdy and Donald joined the pack when they were just two days old. Young birds become closely bonded to whoever they spend time with during their first few days of life. This is called imprinting. When a duckling imprints on someone, she wants to follow them around and be with them all the time. Usually, a duckling imprints on their mother or siblings, but they can also imprint on humans—and dogs!

This is how Rose and Jake became Gerdy and Donald's number one (and two!) pals. As ducklings, Gerdy and Don waddled wherever the pitties roamed. They spent lots of time snuggled up with the dogs, since young ducks need to stay nice and warm. As they grew older, the ducks became more playful, like when Gerdy nibbles on Jake's lip. For this pack, even the silliest things are more fun with friends.

Pitties love vigorous exercise—it's good for the body and brain!

The other animals in this pack include Mia (the kitty); Roxy, Edith, and Helen (the other dogs); several other ducks; and three human siblings.

Ducklings can swim very soon after they hatch.

BUBBLES AND SEAMUS

📍 Laguna,
New South Wales, Australia

From a distance, Bubbles the pig and Seamus the lamb look very much alike. They're both the perfect size for sitting in someone's lap. They're both a light beige color, a bit like the color of milk once all the cereal has been eaten out of it. They both have pink noses, too.

Upon closer inspection, however, their differences are easier to spot. The pig has straight fur that feels wirey to the touch. The lamb has soft, curly fur—perfect for snuggling. And once these animals start moving, you can really tell them apart! Bubbles investigates the farm with purpose, while Seamus moves with more of a bounce, especially when he is excited.

> Pigs don't have many sweat glands, so they sit in mud to keep cool.

Bubbles and Seamus have been the best of pals since they were babies. When they first met, Seamus was nervous. The lamb was born blind, and all the piggy grunting took him by surprise. He had never heard a noise like that! But Seamus soon figured out that wherever Bubbles was, there was usually food. And Seamus likes food!

Bubbles has always taken a protective role toward Seamus. She helps guide her fuzzy friend when he needs it. If Seamus calls out, Bubbles will come running. Then the two of them are off to explore the yard. They'll say hello to the other sheep, try to sneak food out of the other pigs' buckets, and eventually stop for a doze in the sun. What better way to spend the day with your best friend?

Sheep have to be sheared or their wool will keep growing.

PIPPIN AND FRANKENSTEIN

📍 USA

Pippin is a lot like most golden retrievers. She has a fluffy coat of soft fur and a big tongue that pokes out of her mouth when she pants. Pippin is gentle, cheerful, and playful—especially each night when she gets the "zoomies" and races around her house in excitement.

What makes Pippin unique is her unusual "shadow"—otherwise known as Frankenstein the guinea pig! No matter where Pippin is, Frankenstein is close by. If Pippin stretches out for a snooze on the couch, Frank will snuggle under one floppy ear or into her fluffy fur. If Pippin rolls around to scratch her back on the carpet, Frank will creep over to bump noses. And when Pippin trots around in the yard, Frankenstein trots a few steps behind her.

Sometimes Frank forgets about the size difference between him and his best friend. He'll sit so close to Pippin that he'll get whacked by the dog's always wagging tail! But the guinea pig doesn't seem to mind. He likes to be close to his favorite friend no matter what.

Pippin wants to be able to play with Frankenstein at all times, too. Sometimes, the door of the guinea pig's crate will accidentally close, and Pippin will make a fuss until his owner Kayla opens it up again. Kayla knows Pippin would never be the same if they lost track of their little friend. To make sure Frankenstein never gets lost outside, Kayla ties a balloon around his belly so they can always find him!

There are three types of golden retriever: English, American, and Canadian.

Guinea pigs are crepuscular, which means they're most active during dusk and dawn.

BEA AND MIDGE

📍 Vancouver, Canada

Ever since the day they first met, this big dog and little cat have loved to play together. Their favorite game is boxing.

Midge is the troublemaker. She usually starts the match by creeping behind Bea when she is taking a nap. And then it's a swat to Bea's furry snout! Or a swipe to her floppy ear! The dog responds with some playful growls, fake bites, and sometimes a paw to Midge's rear. Then, just as quickly as she started it, Midge will disappear to plot her next attack.

Bea was two years old when she first met eight-week-old Midge. Bea's owner, Bambi, had no plans to add a kitten to their family.

Tuxedo cats like Midge are mostly black with white patches on their chin, chest, belly, and paws.

But when Bambi's friend introduced her to a litter of kittens, little Midge made a big impression. Bea was surprised to find so much ferocity coming from such an itty-bitty kitty. But Bea soon learned to anticipate her tricks—and even love her feisty new playmate! It's a good thing, too, because after so many happy years together, Midge can't stand for Bea to be out of her sight.

In addition to boxing, these furballs love to play their own made-up games, including one Bambi calls "On Button." This game starts when Midge uses one of her tiny paws to press the imaginary "On" button of one of Bea's humongous paws. Then both animals break into happy barks and meows and race around. Whichever game they are playing, these two friends have the most fun when they are together!

Bernese mountain dogs were originally used for herding on farms.

15

ZABU

AND

CAMERON

📍 Tampa, Florida

Zabu and Cameron have spent their entire lives together. Their friendship is extra special because normally these two big cats would never meet each other. In the wild, tigers live in Asia and lions live in Africa—those are totally different continents!

But these big cats didn't meet in the wild. They were raised together in tiny cages at a roadside zoo. That part of their life wasn't easy or happy. Luckily, they had each other.

The two pals were both rescued when they were four years old. Together, they were brought to a big cat sanctuary in Florida. At the sanctuary they got to

A group of tigers is called a streak, and a group of lions is called a pride.

Many white tigers have health problems because of how they are bred for zoos and other attractions.

stay side by side. Sanctuary workers built a large natural enclosure so their unlikely friendship could continue.

These friends both have a special look. Zabu is a white tiger with bright blue eyes. Tigers in the wild are orange, but sadly, some people breed white tigers so they can use them in circuses or at zoos. And Cameron doesn't have a big furry mane like wild lions because he was neutered.

Cameron likes to spend most of the day sleeping—just like lions do in the wild. Zabu, however, is a bundle of energy. She pesters Cameron to play. But he just yawns and rolls over. Eventually, Zabu will give up on Cameron and head to her pool, where she will splash and soak for hours. Another perfect day for these best friends!

Lions are famous for their loud roars—they can be heard up to five miles away.

BUCKET

AND

COLTON

Brodnax, Virginia

Bucket was the smallest calf at a livestock auction when a woman named Susan rescued him. He was only a day old, and they went home together that afternoon.

But there was just one problem. Susan didn't know anything about taking care of a calf. Susan had lots of experience rescuing sheep and goats at Little Buckets Farm Sanctuary, but she had never lived with a cow or bull before. Bucket had been separated from his own mom way too early. Would Susan be able to be a good human mom to this little calf? Soon after she brought little Bucket home, Susan realized he'd need a buddy. That's when Colton the dog came to the rescue.

18

Jersey steers like Bucket are smaller than most other types of cattle.

Susan slowly introduced the two animals. Soon, Colton and Bucket were inseparable. They made the perfect pair. For starters, the dog and the calf were almost exactly the same size. (Now Bucket is much bigger, though!) Bucket and Colton have similar personalities, too. They both love being silly, getting pet, and *racing*.

Lots of cows like to run and play as much as Bucket does, but most cows don't have a dog as a best friend! Colton's favorite game is tag, and his favorite partner is Bucket. They run and chase each other all over the sanctuary. Sometimes, Bucket can even outrun Colton. For a cow, he runs and gallops pretty fast.

After they race, Bucket and Colton take turns doing their other favorite thing: chewing gently on each other's ears!

Most dogs can run around 15 miles per hour—but some can reach speeds of up to 45 miles per hour!

YODA AND LILY

At first glance, a miniature donkey and a long-haired Chihuahua don't seem to have that much in common. For one thing, they are completely different sizes. A Chihuahua is only about the size of a donkey's head!

Donkeys and Chihuahuas usually have very different personalities, too. Donkeys tend to be careful animals. This makes many people think they are stubborn. Chihuahuas are the opposite. These pocket-sized pups have big-dog attitude and the courage to match.

Despite these differences, Lily the donkey and Yoda the Chihuahua are best buds. From the minute he first saw her, Yoda was curious about Lily. The donkey was patient with Yoda. She didn't seem to mind that there was a tiny dog investigating her every move.

Once the two animals got to know each other a little better, Yoda seemed to have an idea. He wanted to *ride* his new donkey friend! Their human, Laura, made sure this idea was okay with Lily. Then she came up with a clever way for Yoda to climb aboard Lily's back. Laura found a step stool that was just the right size for Yoda to hop from the ground to the stool to Lily's back. Then it was time to ride!

These days, Yoda happily sits on his donkey friend as Lily slowly moves around the yard, finding the best bits of grass to chomp on. Lily seems to like it just as much. It turns out these two friends have a lot in common after all!

Chihuahuas are the world's smallest dog breed.

Male donkeys are called "jacks," and females are "jennets."

21

TOMMY

AND JACK

📍 Ontario, Canada

Tommy is a speedy Canadian red squirrel. In many ways, Tommy is pretty normal. He loves to munch on nuts, burrow to keep warm, and chatter to let others know how he feels. But Tommy has some trouble walking and balancing, so he was rescued by his humans, Mel and Will. Now he lives inside with his best friend, Jack, a ginger tabby cat who's six times his size!

Jack was also a rescue animal in need of some TLC. Unlike Tommy, Jack is very calm. Before Tommy came along, Jack's main hobbies included sleeping in a patch of sunshine, hiding in a paper bag, and batting around a pinecone. But now that Tommy's part of the family, Jack's life is much more action-packed! These days, the ginger cat divides his time between playfully sneaking up on

A group of cats can be called a clowder and a group of squirrels can be called a scurry.

his bushy-tailed squirrel friend and making sure Tommy stays out of trouble when they're playing outside.

These best friends act just like brothers. Sometimes, Tommy makes Jack mad, like when he grabs onto Jack's paw and won't let go! But most of the time, Tommy just follows Jack wherever he goes. If Jack heads to the scratching post to give his claws a workout, Tommy does laps around it. If Jack lounges in his chair, Tommy hops in for a snuggle. And when Jack stops by his food bowl, Tommy isn't far behind. No matter where they are, this cat loves having a little squirrel shadow.

Squirrels and cats both communicate with their tails.

What happens when a 100-pound golden retriever named Barclay and a 6-pound white Pekin duck named Rudy meet? They become besties—eventually.

Their friendship got off to a slow start the day Barclay's human, Pam, brought home a group of ducks. The ducks settled in right away, flapping here and quacking there. They were happy to be a part of the family! Barclay, however, wasn't so sure.

Even though Barclay had his doubts, Rudy knew right away that Barclay was the dog for him. If Rudy caught sight of Barclay, Rudy would waddle toward him. But if Barclay caught sight of Rudy, he'd run away!

Eventually, though, Barclay's curiosity got the better of him. While Barclay was investigating Rudy—and his snacks—Rudy started investigating Barclay. He hopped up on Barclay's back and started grooming his hair. And Barclay liked it!

USA

BARCLAY AND RUDY

Ducks dip hard food into water to make it soft enough to swallow.

Ever since that day, the two friends do *everything* together. The first thing Barclay does after he wakes up is check the duck coop. If his orange-billed buddies are taking a bath, Barclay patiently sits with them and sometimes takes a sip of their bathwater. If Barclay is eating lunch, he makes sure to share with Rudy. Barclay even stays nearby when the ducks are going to the bathroom!

Playing is good, but napping is better. Rudy helps Barclay fall asleep by nipping and grooming his soft fur until the pup has drifted off. Then, Rudy snuggles down for a nap, too.

Dogs watch humans' body language to figure out how people feel.

HOPE AND MEADOW

Hope the cat and Meadow the dog may be two of the most well-traveled animal siblings on the planet. When Hope was just a kitten, she stopped traffic by wandering onto a busy bridge in Charleston, South Carolina. Luckily, a local animal shelter saved her, cleaned her up, and helped her find a forever home.

Hope's new human sister was a fifth grader, and they got to grow up together. When Hope's sister became an adult and graduated college, Hope went to live with her. Soon after that, they decided to hit the road together! Hope and her new family set off on an RV journey across the United States. Hope spent so much time traveling that she earned the title, "Queen of the Campground." After their road trip was over, they headed to the West Indies. Soon, Hope had two new titles: "Queen of the Caribbean" and big sister!

The Chihuahua is named after the Mexican state of Chihuahua.

Hope's owner had adopted Meadow, a long-haired Chihuahua covered in polka dots. When Meadow first came home, she was sick. She needed to be nursed back to health. But once the puppy was feeling better, she was excited to get to know her new cat sibling.

At first, Hope ignored Meadow. But Meadow kept trying. She chased Hope, buried her face into Hope's belly, and cuddled her. Eventually, Hope learned to love her energetic little friend. Now Hope and Meadow have so much fun play-fighting, taking naps, sunbathing, and napping together. But their favorite thing is still traveling the world. Next stop: Europe!

Cats with stripes that run across their spines are called mackerel tabbies.

RALPHY

AND BUCKLEY

Latrobe, California

When Buckley was just a calf, he was separated from his mom. Soon after, he was adopted by a woman named Leslie. But Buckley was so lonely that he cried for three days straight. Leslie hoped that the other animals on her farm could be a comfort to the little calf. Instead, they pushed Buckley around.

Unlike most animals, goats have rectangular pupils.

Leslie was so worried about Buckley that she even spent a night sleeping in the barn with him. Then, Leslie found out about another orphaned animal named Ralphy who needed a home. Could a baby goat be a friend to a baby bull? There was only one way to find out.

At first, the baby Nubian goat was terrified. Buckley was more than twice Ralphy's size! But Leslie wasn't ready to give up. She coaxed Ralphy into a neighboring pen so the two could get to know each other but still have some personal space. After a few days, Leslie found Buckley and Ralphy sleeping side by side, their furry bodies pressed together between the fence. After that, the Nubian goat and the Highland calf were inseparable.

With Ralphy by his side, Buckley was a brand-new calf. He was full of energy—and surprisingly bouncy, despite his massive size! Leslie was thrilled to see the two galloping around the farm together, even if they were kicking over wheelbarrows and bags of food! These rascals also enjoy rolling giant exercise balls around and racing home to get a handful of sweet crunchy grapes from their human mom.

The coat of Highland cattle can grow 13 inches long.

For a long time, Rudy the pig was an only child. He got to do pretty much anything he wanted, whenever he wanted. That included dancing and snuggling with his mom, Kate; going for four-wheeler rides; and even sneaking a sip of Kate's drinks! Rudy didn't think life could get much better.

Then one day, he got a new little brother, a kitten named Mr. Feeny. When Kate first rescued Feeny, he was sick. His leg was badly hurt and he needed lots of extra care. Luckily, Feeny got better. Soon he felt good enough to hang out with Rudy! Teeny Feeny never let Rudy out of his sight. He wanted Rudy to stay close, where he could rub up against his snout, his head, or his back. Wherever Rudy was, Feeny was nearby.

RUDY AND THE CATS

📍 USA

Then Kate got *another* cat, a frisky white kitten with an orange-ish tail and ears. His name was Little Willie, and he was much wilder than his older brothers. Little Willie thinks Rudy's swishing tail is the perfect toy! When Little Willie isn't sitting on Rudy's back or trying to grab his tail, the kitten is playfully chewing on Rudy's ears.

Now that Rudy lives with two cats, he never has any time to himself. His brothers are always following him around and stealing his sunny spots. But that's just the way Rudy likes it. With best friends like this, life definitely can't get any better.

LINK AND BENJI

📍 USA

"**F**riends that flop together, stay together." That's one of the ways Benji and Link's human mom describes their unique friendship. And it's true: This odd couple spends a lot of time flopping around together. They'll flop on their owner's soft bed, across the smooth hardwood floor, and outside in a big field of bright green grass. After all, having this much fun together can be exhausting!

Benji is a brown-and-white lop-eared rabbit. His hobbies include chewing holes in his owner's shirts, begging for snacks, and playing with his best friend's tail.

Link is a caramel-colored golden retriever. Like most golden retrievers, Link has always been affectionate with the little animals in his family. His first tiny friend was a hamster named Kirby. They got along so well that his owner knew Link

Rabbits can eat small amounts of veggies and fruits for a treat, but their diet mainly consists of hay.

would be okay with a little rabbit like Benji, too.

Benji was a bit nervous when he first met the big dog. But that didn't last very long. Benji's curiosity took over. He wanted to know more about Link—especially his super fluffy tail! Benji loves to try and catch it, or wake Link up from a nap with some nose kisses. The little rabbit also gets into trouble by stealing Link's toys. When he finds a good one, Benji will "chin" it, which means rubbing his chin all over the toy to claim it as his own.

Link is happy to share his toys—and tail!—with a friend as good as Benji.

Two presidents have had golden retrievers in the White House: President Ford (Liberty and Misty) and President Reagan (Victory).

BARON AND ALVIN

📍 Chandler, Arizona

Baron and Alvin spend lots of time relaxing on the bed, curled up together as close as can be. Baron, a sweet German shepherd with long pointy ears, gets to be the big spoon. He hops on his bed and curls himself into a comfy position. Then his kitty brother scooches in.

These best friends got along as soon as they met. But their close friendship was put to the test when Baron starting having seizures. Baron's seizures were scary for him and for his family. But luckily, Alvin was brave and knew just what to do to help his friend.

34

After one of Baron's seizures, Alvin jumped up to Baron's side and began to comfort him with his scratchy pink tongue. Alvin started to gently and firmly lick Baron's long snout. Then he moved over to the dog's soft ears. The kitty kept licking for as long as it took Baron to feel better.

During the lick therapy, Baron sat perfectly still. His owner, Eliza, said it was like he was in a trance. It was clear to Eliza that Baron found Alvin's "grooming" soothing and relaxing. Even though Baron's seizures have since stopped, he still likes being licked by Alvin. In fact, the dog likes it so much that Baron will now plop down in front of Alvin, tilt his head up, and wait for a grooming session. Thanks, friend!

CHARLIE AND DORA

📍 Ontario, Canada

Dora keeps tabs on all the animals at the Happy Tails Farm Sanctuary. The calico cat walks along the top of the pigpen to make sure everyone is behaving, and she flops on top of the rabbit hutch to check on the bunnies. But her favorite place to hang out is in the sheep pen where her best friend, Charlie, lives.

These two have been friends ever since they were both rescued as babies. Dora was just a few weeks old when Carla, the sanctuary owner, found her. The tiny kitten was wet and shivering in the cold November air. Carla warmed her up, got her home, and carefully fed her through a medicine dropper. Luckily, Dora regained her strength just in time to help another animal in need. That animal was Charlie.

Charlie was orphaned soon after he was born. He needed a lot of hands-on care from the people at the animal sanctuary—and from his new friend, Dora. The cat came over to give Charlie a sniff as soon as he arrived. Dora must have thought Charlie smelled pretty good, because then she nuzzled his head and licked his nose. From that moment on, the two were inseparable.

The two best friends spend their days grooming each other, sharing bites of hay, and getting into lots of trouble. And now that Charlie lives outside, they like to take turns visiting each other and exploring the farm together.

FRANKIE AND MAGGIE

Most people have heard of a guard dog, but not too many have ever met a guard *goat*. It turns out that goats like Frankie have an excellent built-in alarm system for protecting their family: spitting! Her owners, Cate and Chad, learned all about it on one of their daily hikes. That's when Frankie warned them about a mama bear and her cubs who were walking nearby.

Frankie would do just about anything for her crew, especially her best friend, Maggie, a senior cocker spaniel. Maggie can't hear anymore, so Frankie is always there to help the dog figure out what's going on. These two animals love exploring the world together in the Airstream trailer where they live. Even though there is plenty of room to spread out, Maggie and Frankie usually sleep right on top of each other. When they're ready to sightsee during their travels, they stick their

Goats can eat most plants, including some that are poisonous to people, like poison ivy.

heads out of the same window and let the breeze ruffle their fur.

Outside their trailer, Frankie and Maggie love to explore. They've traveled 40,000 miles across the country with their humans, hiking through more than 25 states and camping in countless national parks. Their favorite destination is in central California where Maggie and Frankie love to leap from rock to rock and investigate shady crevices. The next day they might be running along a beach, sniffing plants in the desert, or wandering through a stream. Where will this odd couple go next?

You can train dogs who are deaf to respond to hand signals and flashlights.

ELWAY AND STOUT

📍 Stonington, CT

Best friends Elway and Stout live with five big dogs on a Connecticut farm. Just like the big dogs, these two little animals play with toys, take walks on leashes, and end the day by flopping on a comfy dog bed.

This makes sense for Stout, a tiny black Chihuahua. For Elway, this behavior is a little more unusual. Elway is black like Stout, wags his tail like Stout, and wears a collar like Stout. But Elway is a duck, not a dog!

Elway was just four weeks old when he first met his Chihuahua best friend. At the time, Stout was still a baby, too. The two of them were the smallest members of their pack, so they grew up looking out for each other. Ever since then, wherever Stout goes, Elway goes, too. Dog birthday party? There's Elway! A dip in the pool? Elway's first in line. This laidback duck and gentle Chihuahua do pretty much everything together.

There's only one place that Elway goes without Stout: the hospital. But Elway isn't sick. He's a therapy duck! On therapy days, Elway wears his best collar and leash and heads off to do his rounds. At the hospital he waddles down the hall cheering up patients or sitting with them while they have lunch. Elway's not very good at applying bandages, but he's still a pretty decent nurse!

Once he returns home, Elway and Stout get back to playing, cuddling, and being the best of friends.

Chihuahuas usually weigh less than 6 pounds.

Ducks blow bubbles underwater to clean out dirt and food from their nostrils.

41

HELEN, UMA, AND OLIVER

Scio, Oregon

H elen is a big bison with a shaggy coat of thick, snuggly fur. Like all American bison, Helen has an excellent sense of hearing and smell. But Helen was born blind.

Helen lives on a six-acre pasture at Lighthouse Farm Sanctuary with around 200 other rescued animals. But when she first got there, Helen would keep to herself. Gwen, who runs the sanctuary, could tell that Helen was a bit lonely. All that changed when a calf named Oliver was born.

Meeting Oliver completely changed Helen's personality. Helen wasn't skittish anymore. Now, Helen groomed Oliver and acted like a second mother to him. And it wasn't just Oliver. Soon, Helen started welcoming each and every new

animal to the sanctuary, whether they were a spunky hen, a shy lamb, or a noisy pig.

But one noisy pig in particular formed a special bond with Helen. Helen met Uma when the pig was just a baby. Gwen kept a close eye on them. After all, Uma was so tiny, and Helen couldn't see the little pig when she weaved between the big bison's feet. But Helen could hear and smell Uma, and that was good enough.

Now, instead of Gwen keeping an eye on Uma, Uma keeps an eye on Helen. She trots around Helen, making sure that none of the big steers get too close, chattering away the whole time. And at night, Uma snuggles up in Helen's hay so the two friends can have a sleepover under the stars.

EMMA

AND

ELMO

USA

Elmo the cat used to live a life of noise, confusion, and chaos. His first home had too many cats, too many dogs, and too many kids. All the commotion made it hard for Elmo to relax.

Luckily, he found a new home with Karen and Tina. His new humans only had one animal at home: a sweet dog named Emma. They thought that Elmo

Favorite way to drink: out of a TALL glass of water . . . with ice!

would find it easy to live with just *one* dog, especially one who was calm and quiet.

But, when Elmo arrived, he spent a lot of time hiding from his new pit bull sibling. Emma was patient, though. If Elmo wanted to hide *under* the bed, Emma would bring her toys *next* to the bed. If Elmo wanted to stay out of reach on the windowsill, Emma rolled on the floor *under* the windowsill. After a few months, no one thought Emma and Elmo would ever be friends.

Luckily, they were all wrong. It turned out that Emma and Elmo were just keeping their friendship a secret! When Tina and Karen were at work, the two animals snuggled on the couch. But, as soon as they heard the front door open, Emma and Elmo would each bolt off the couch and out of the room. Nothing to see here!

Eventually, Elmo and Emma let everyone know that they were best friends. They were having too much fun wrestling on the floor and cuddling on the couch to break up the party when someone came home.

Favorite way to drink: out of Emma's glass!

A group of kittens can be called a litter—and so can a group of puppies.

JUNE AND WAFFLES

📍 Arkansas

June was just a couple of days old when a woman named Bethany found her crying in her backyard. The little raccoon had gotten separated from her family. She was so small and cold. Bethany knew it was up to her to take care of the baby raccoon. With lots of love, nurturing, and frozen blueberries, June grew stronger—and more mischievous! Bethany thought June could use an older sister to keep her from getting into too much trouble.

That's when Bethany adopted Waffles, a sweet vizsla with a golden-rust coat. After a few getting-to-know-you sniffs, the two animals started racing around the yard in their very own made-up game. Outside, these friends do lots of running and jumping. Inside, they love to wrestle and snuggle up together on the couch.

The only time they stop playing is when they pause for a snack. Waffles is happy to share, but June would rather have the whole bowl to herself!

But even though these two sisters spend all their time together, they're very different. June is very energetic and can get a little wild. Raccoons are curious animals, and June gets her tiny paws into everything. She'll climb into the sink, nap in a sock drawer, and pry open the trash can to see what's inside. She doesn't like anything to be closed! Luckily, she has Waffles to keep an eye on her. Waffles is the more responsible of the two. She's an independent dog who loves attention—especially from her best friend!

Wild raccoons eat fruits, seeds, birds' eggs, insects, frogs, and plants.

Vizslas are great jogging and biking buddies.

SAPPHIRA AND

COCO

Coco and Sapphira live in Denmark, a country known for brightly colored houses, tall ships, and elaborate castles. But this odd couple doesn't do much sightseeing. They are too busy looking for their human mom's snacks!

Coco is a mini lop-eared brown rabbit covered in white patches. According to her human, Coco is a bit bossy and completely obsessed with food. She especially loves fruit, like bananas, watermelon, and even a few apples from her mom's plate!

Sapphira is a breed of cat called a Birman. Just like most Birmans, Sapphira has long silky fur. Sapphira also has bright blue eyes. That's how she got her name—her eyes are the same color as blue sapphires. According to her human, Sapphira is a bit of a clumsy cat and completely obsessed with her bunny best friend.

Sapphira will happily spend her afternoon grooming Coco, licking her soft ears and wiggly nose. Coco happily takes the licks, but she doesn't usually return them. Maybe she is more worried about hairballs than her buddy is! When these siblings aren't snuggling, they are getting into trouble—especially Sapphira! The little kitty has been known to hide her mom's keys, rip open bags of treats, and destroy rolls of toilet paper in the bathroom. Sapphira is extra clumsy, too. Once she tried to jump up to grab a treat and instead broke a shelf and two drawers in the closet! But whatever mess Sapphira is getting into, you can be sure that Coco is right by her side.

A female rabbit is called a doe, and a male rabbit is called a buck.

Birman kittens are born white. Their color comes in as they get older.

49

TK AND THE NAUGHTY DOG BRIGADE

Nashville, Tennessee

Cats can make around 100 different sounds.

The day a woman named Anneliessa rescued an eight-week-old kitten, she knew she was doing the cat a favor. After all, the kitten had been huddled on the side of the road with cars zooming by. Still, Anneliessa was nervous. The kitten was only about the size of a bagel, and Anneliessa had three dogs. She called them the "Naughty Dog Brigade" because their playing often turned mischievous. Once, Anneliessa had come home to find her bedroom covered in feathers—the naughty dogs had shredded every pillow in the room! She wasn't sure if the trio had ever been around a cat before.

Shelter dogs learn how to socialize by going on walks with volunteers.

Anneliessa decided to name the little ball of fluff Tiny Kitten, or TK for short. TK spent the first day in her new home cuddled snuggly inside her cat carrier while the dogs investigated the unfamiliar animal inside. Eventually, Anneliessa carefully introduced TK to Nera, the grumpiest of her dogs. Nera had always been the boss of the group, so her reaction mattered. Nera sniffed TK's head, she sniffed TK's tail, and then she fell in love.

The other two dogs, Fred and Willow, quickly fell in love with TK, too. They especially liked her special kitty licks. TK treats each of her dog friends to daily grooming, using her scratchy pink tongue to clean each dog's face and ears.

These four rescued animals are happy to have a safe place to snuggle on the couch, look out the window, and chase each other around the yard. What lucky friends!

51

OSKAR AND XANTHIPPE

📍 Eureka, California

Xanthippe has always had three favorite activities: cooling down in a wading pool, getting belly scratches from her human mom, Thommie, and getting kisses from her dog best friend, Oskar.

Oskar started giving the piglet kisses as soon as he met her. Thommie brought Xanthippe home because her pig mom wasn't taking care of her. Xanthippe was just a few hours old and smaller than a loaf of bread. Oskar's head was bigger than her entire body!

Even though the bulldog was a lot bigger than the piglet, Xan was never afraid of him. Instead, Xanthippe quickly came to think of Oskar as her mom—probably because Oskar started giving her some love as soon as she joined the family.

First, Oskar gave the piglet a good bath. He licked every part of her, from her pink snout to her curly black tail. Just like a piggy mama would! Then, he helped Xanthippe learn to walk. Before Oskar showed her how, she didn't know how to use her hind legs.

Soon the two friends were racing around the yard and playing hide-and-seek in big piles of hay. When it was time for a break, Oskar and Xanthippe would relax on Oskar's doggy bed. After a nap, Xanthippe would start another round of playing, climbing, and jumping all over Oskar.

These days, Xanthippe is a lot bigger than Oskar—much too big to climb all over him—but the two friends still cuddle up together and go on nice, slow walks.

Xanthippe is a kunekune, a small pig breed from New Zealand.

BRADY AND TUUKKA

White cats are often deaf, but not Tuukka.

Ventura, California

Meet Brady and Tuukka, animal siblings who wrestle day and night. Their humans, Taryn and Jenna, refer to their two wrestlers as "the dogs." But only *one* of the furballs technically holds that title!

Brady is a sunny-colored golden retriever with soft, wavy fur. His favorite hobbies include eating peanut butter, lying in the sun, and chewing the biggest sticks he can find.

Tuukka is a brilliant-white cat who *thinks* she's a dog. After all, she was raised by Brady! When Tuukka isn't starting a round of wrestling, she enjoys sneaking through the garden, chewing grass, and snoozing in her cat perch on the backyard door.

These two buddies met when Tuukka was adopted as a small kitten. To help her adjust to her new home—and the big dog who lived there—Taryn and Jenna started off by keeping the two animals apart. Each animal had their own room, connected by a sliding glass door. While Tuukka slowly explored her room, Brady sat right at the door, peering in at the little kitten.

Tuukka seemed to have no problem with the species difference. In fact, Tuukka even tried to nurse from her doggy friend. Brady didn't mind. He just helped Tuukka quench her thirst in a water bowl instead. To this day, Tuukka only drinks water out of a giant dog bowl.

These best friends spend all their time together, wrestling and playing and exploring outside. But, at the end of the day, there's nothing better than snuggling together.

Golden retrievers love to swim.

BILLO AND AVNI

Dharamshala, India

On a normal day, you can probably find Avni, a young rhesus macaque monkey, doing one of three things: wrestling with puppies, teasing some sheep, or carefully grooming her best friend, Billo the cat.

Billo is a gentle tabby who lives at Peepal Farm. Everyone there agrees that Billo is the kindest kitty they've ever met. She helped Avni when the baby monkey needed it most.

Avni came to Peepal Farm after she had been hurt and separated from her family. Her arm was in bad shape, and she had to have it removed. Being injured and alone was scary and stressful for the baby primate. Luckily, Billo stepped in. She comforted Avni with lots of attention and some much needed snuggling. This helped Avni heal faster.

A group of cats can be called a glaring and a group of monkeys can be called a barrel.

Becoming friends with Billo helped Avni gain the confidence to spend time with other animals on the farm, too. She especially likes playing with the puppies— and stealing their sticks!

Once Avni recovered from her injury, she was released back into the wild. Avni was excited to spend her days in the treetops where she was born. But she couldn't stay away from the rescue farm—she missed Billo too much. Now Avni makes daily visits to her best friend. Avni finds Billo wherever she might be snoozing and gently strokes her whiskers and grooms her fur. Billo helped Avni learn to be as kind and compassionate as she was.

Many kinds of animals—including cats and monkeys—groom one another as a way to bond and show friendship.

DODGER, MONTY, AND IKE

 Milton, Florida

The brown spots above Dodger's eyes are known as kiss marks.

The minute Dodger's human mom, Brandi, saw him, she knew he was special. Brandi met the puppy when he was just a few weeks old. She noticed him right away because he was so small! Brandi decided she needed to take him home. She was so happy for this beautiful dog to become part of her family.

After adopting Dodger, Brandi adopted two rats, Monty and Ike. Brandi calls Monty "a lazy bum" and Ike "the spitfire." Soon all three animals became best friends. When Monty is with Dodger, they like to cuddle. When Ike is with Dodger, they play with tennis balls. Sometimes Ike tries to steal Dodger's toys—even though they are bigger than he is!

When these three friends play, Dodger rolls over onto his back. This shows the rats that Dodger wants to play with them, not hunt them! Dodger certainly is big enough to eat the rats, but he would never hurt his brothers. Instead, he sits perfectly still while Monty and Ike race up his back and leap from his head. Then Dodger rolls over to let the little rats investigate his ears.

Sometimes Dodger acts like *he* is a rat, too. It seems like he would like nothing more than to climb into the rats' cage when they go to bed for the night. But the dog is much too big for that! Instead, Dodger invites Monty and Ike to join him for games on his dog bed. That way there's plenty of room for everyone!

Monty's and Ike's fur has a caped pattern: a mostly white body with a colored head and a back stripe.

Edna and Thomas live with about 150 other farm animals at a sprawling animal sanctuary in Australia. But these two don't have much else in common! Edna is a pig. She is calm, mature, and very smart. Edna is content to spend her days quietly, munching on a pear here and enjoying some watermelon there. When she does speak, it is a single grunt or two, usually to say how happy she is to be showered with a hose.

Thomas the duck, however, is not calm *or* quiet. No one ever has to wonder where Thomas is—you can hear him from a mile away! He is always quacking about something and running around the farm.

It took some time for this mismatched pair to become friends. First, Thomas visited Edna's pen. When the pig didn't send him away, the duck took it as an invitation to come back! He started joining her for breakfast. Then he was sitting with Edna while she dozed. Each time he visited, Thomas crept a little closer. As soon as Edna allowed him to sit right next to her, he decided he was allowed to climb up and sit on her back! The rest is history.

THOMAS AND EDNA

Laguna,
New South Wales, Australia

Pigs greet each other by rubbing noses.

These days, Thomas's favorite activity is guarding Edna—even though the pig weighs more than 200 pounds! The little duck struts back and forth, quacking with authority, and chasing after any little pig or shy hen who wanders too close to his best friend. He always has her back!

Blood moves through a duck's feet in a special way that keeps them from getting frostbite.

OLLIE, LEO, AND RIZZY

Long Island, NY

Leo and Ollie are cheerful golden retrievers who always seem to have smiles on their faces. During the summer, Leo is smiling whenever he's near the water. That means racing along the beach, leaping into a swimming pool, or even relaxing on an oversized pool float. During the winter, Ollie smiles when he's bounding through the snow. But no matter what time of year it is, both dogs' smiles are biggest when they're snuggling with their best friend, Rizzy the cat.

Rizzy was the first animal to join the family. She was a stray who had a bad eye infection when she was first rescued. With help from the local vet and some TLC from her new family, Rizzy started to feel better. But she still has some trouble with her eyes, like telling how far away things are. But Rizzy doesn't let this slow her down. She is a feisty cat who likes to be where the action is. That usually means wherever her buddies Ollie and Leo are.

These three are such good friends that they even share toys. Leo will parade around with one of Rizzy's cat toys. Rizzy does the same with Leo's stuffed bunnies. She'll drag one to his dog bed and snuggle with it. But the dogs themselves are Rizzy's favorite toys. Rizzy loves to chew on the pups' fluffy paws and cheeks. Neither of them mind. In fact, Leo will walk over to her window seat so Rizzy can chomp away.

Adult cats usually weigh around 10 pounds, but some larger breeds can be twice that!

ARI AND

LILLY

📍 Alabama

The first time Ari and Lilly met, they weren't so sure about each other. After all, Ari was a big, 12-year-old husky, and Lilly was a small, 2-year-old rabbit. So Ari and Lilly took it slow. They eyed each other from across the room. They sniffed noses through Lilly's rabbit hutch. But pretty soon, the two fuzzballs overlooked their age and size differences and became the best of friends.

Even though they have different kinds of diets, Ari and Lilly love to share food. After Lilly finishes her own dinner, she hops over to Ari's food bowl to see if the dog has left her a bite or two. If no one's looking, Lilly will try and slide Ari's bowl across the floor and under the couch, so she can snack in peace. Other times, the two of them will drink from the same water bowl, Ari's big husky head right over Lilly's bunny one.

Friends like these also look out for each other. Once, Lilly was exploring for a really long time. Ari thought her bunny friend might be stuck, so she whimpered and howled until their humans came to get Lilly out of her hiding spot. Lilly looks out for her big sister, too. The bunny waits by the door to make sure the husky comes back from her evening strolls safe and sound.

And of course, the friends love cuddling. Lilly uses Ari as a big pillow and gently licks Ari's nose, paws, and ears. It's her way of saying, "I'm glad we're friends!"

65

Zach was just a few weeks old when a hurricane blew him out of a tree. The hurricane made it difficult to get this kit (another name for a baby squirrel) to a trained wildlife rehabilitator. Luckily, a man named Dave found out about the baby squirrel.

Dave had experience rescuing squirrels. He had everything he needed to take care of the little guy. Dave woke up every few hours to feed Zach with a tiny eye-dropper and make sure he was warm and safe.

ZACH AND HIS DOGS

Squirrel Appreciation Day is January 21.

 Florida

There were a few others around to help take care of Zach: two curious golden retrievers named Maddox and Madison. They were very concerned about the baby squirrel. They gave him lots of kisses and nuzzles as he was growing up. And when Zach was older, the big dogs let him ride around on their backs, climb in their fur, and even nibble on their paws.

Zach loves his big brother and sister, but when Dave got a new puppy named Major, Zach knew he had found his best friend. Major and Zach love running around and playing together. Major follows the little squirrel around wherever he goes. He even seems to want to follow Zach up the curtains when they play hide-and-seek! Zach likes to groom Major and give him little kisses on his nose. But Major's favorite thing to do is slurp up the crumbs once Zach finishes a snack. Yum!

International Golden Retriever Day is February 3.

COASTER AND BUTTERCUP

📍 Woodinville, Washington

The first time Buttercup and Coaster met, things didn't go quite as planned. Coaster, a 13-year-old horse, had recently moved to a new farm and was having trouble settling in. Changes of any sort can be tricky to get used to, and this show horse had moved all the way across the country! She liked to compete and win ribbons, but she was having trouble making friends.

Luckily, the people at her new home had an idea. What if they introduced Coaster to a young goat? Goats have sweet personalities and make good therapy animals for people and animals. And there was a baby goat nearby who needed rescuing. Everyone thought it was a good idea—everyone except Coaster.

Horses can sleep both lying down and standing up.

During Coaster and Buttercup's first few meetings, the horse was pretty cranky. So Buttercup started visiting other horses around the farm. That made Coaster a little jealous, and she seemed to rethink her behavior.

Eventually, the two animals discovered that they had a lot in common. Now they spend all of their time together! The goat even goes with Coaster when she travels to different competitions. On the road, the two animals don't need any extra space. That's because Buttercup is usually standing directly under Coaster—or sitting across her back while she lies down. Now the only time either animal gets cranky is when they have to be separated. Friends stick together!

There are more than 200 different breeds of goat.

A group of horses can be called a team, and a group of goats can be called a tribe.

MISTO, SAUVE,

AND BOGART

📍 Chesapeake, Virginia

Misto and Sauve spend their days getting into all sorts of trouble, and then looking innocent—even if you catch them in the act!

These two mischief makers are sphynx cats. That makes them energetic cats with excellent balance. Misto and Sauve are often found perched on top of a bookcase or on their humans' shoulders!

Like many cats, sphynxes love to be around humans and other animals. Misto and Sauve are no different. These cats' favorite companion is the family dog, Bogart the boxer. Like many boxers, Bogart is playful and has a great sense of humor. He's also patient, which makes him great with the cats! Bogart puts up with all of Misto and Sauve's shenanigans, whether they are leaping at him from behind the couch, nibbling on his ears, or just teasing him.

It's probably good for Bogart that he spends part of his day at doggy day care. There, in the company of other dogs, he is the boss! But as soon as he returns home, the cats are in charge again. First things first: Sauve rushes over to sniff Bogart's feet! Sauve won't rest until he has investigated all the new smells on Bogart's paws and rubbed all over him so everyone knows Bogart is *his* dog! Misto is more playful. She likes to wrestle with Bogart, acting like a little tiger as she pretends to bite Bogart's throat.

Sphynx cats are famous for their wrinkly, furless bodies.

Bogart happily plays along, and returns a few fake bites of his own. All is good between these funny friends!

Boxers are often used as guide dogs for the blind.

QUASI AND PONGO

In the wild, squirrels often dart up trees and dig in dirt and leaves to bury a nut. In this home, however, Quasi the squirrel tries to bury a nut under the belly of Pongo the dog! Pongo doesn't mind. The basset hound probably figures it's all part of taking care of a squirrel baby. As far as Pongo is concerned, he became Quasi's dad the day he saved his life.

When Quasi was just four weeks old, he fell out of his nest. It might have been because he was born partially blind or because the hump on his back made it difficult for him to balance in the tree. Luckily, Quasi's fall happened in Pongo's backyard. As soon as Pongo spotted the baby squirrel, he started to bark and bark and bark. The dog kept barking until his owner came over. Pongo and his human knew they had to help this baby squirrel.

Pongo took his role as Quasi's caretaker very seriously. He watched as his human used a soft towel to warm the tiny squirrel. He inched closer as his human used a tiny medicine dropper to feed the squirrel. Even after Quasi recovered from his fall and got a little bigger, Pongo still thinks of himself as Quasi's protector.

Pongo and Quasi have plenty of playtime, too. Pongo loves to watch Quasi race around the house. And they have even more fun when Quasi jumps onto Pongo's back for a doggy ride. Go, Pongo, go!

MOKI AND HER GUINEA PIGS

San Francisco, California

Every good friend knows that sharing is caring. That's why Moki shares her bed, her toys, and her kisses with her best pals—even though Moki's toys are *bigger* than her friends. That's because Moki is a pit bull terrier and her two best friends are guinea pigs.

Moki used to live at an animal shelter. She had never seen a guinea pig. But her new owner, Kris, had two guinea pigs at home, Frida and Pandora. The shelter

American pit bull terriers like Moki have lots of energy and are known for being very loyal.

workers warned Kris to keep the little animals in their cage around Moki. No one knew how the pit bull terrier would react to these unfamiliar animals.

Frida and Pandora had never seen a dog before, either. The guinea pigs' first instinct was to freeze when they saw the pit bull. Maybe if they ignored Moki, she would go away. But the big dog came even closer. When Frida moved left, Moki's eyes followed. When Pandora moved right, Moki's ears went up.

Moki was desperate to investigate these critters! So she slowly moved toward their crate and sniffed. Eventually, Frida and Pandora waddled over and gave Moki a sniff of their own. Moki's response? A big wet kiss—with a tongue that was nearly half the size of their bodies!

Ever since then, the trio is always together. Moki will sometimes use Pandora as a pillow, and Frida will sometimes use Moki as a bed. And although Moki always offers her toys to her buddies, they would rather snuggle with their giant friend instead.

A male guinea pig is called a boar and female is called a sow.

MAMIAO AND HONEY

📍 Thailand

Honey and Mamiao love any day when they get to take a long stroll along the water with their human family. For a long time, Mamiao, a friendly golden retriever, was the only animal on these walks. But one day, Mamiao's humans found Honey, a tiny ginger cat, and brought him home.

Honey had been living on the streets, scrambling for meals, hiding from the rain, and, unfortunately, sometimes getting hurt. The cat wasn't used to people, other animals, or even being cared for. So when Honey came to live with Mamiao, walking along the water was the last thing on his mind. Honey had a broken tail, and he needed to heal.

Mamiao was the perfect pal to help Honey recover and get used to living with his new family. Mamiao started the welcoming process by giving Honey lots of big licks. At the time, Honey was almost smaller than Mamiao's tongue! Then

Mamiao
is also the name
of a town in
China.

Mamiao snuggled up around Honey for naps. Soon, Honey felt right at home with his new big sister.

Once Honey healed, grooming and cuddling turned into playing and wrestling. Now, Honey likes to leap in and out of boxes while Mamiao barks encouragement. Sometimes Honey gets cozy in a basket. When that happens, Mamiao picks up the basket and carries it around with Honey inside! Sometimes they even let their human family dress them up in silly hats for photos. As long as these best friends are together, anything can be fun!

Ginger cats
are almost
always male.

GALAXY AND BERNIE

What has two tails, four ears, and is covered in kisses? A Bernie and Galaxy snuggle sandwich, of course! Bernie and Galaxy are a rat and cat duo who live in New York City. The first time they met, their humans were pretty nervous. What if the two animals didn't get along?

Luckily, Galaxy took one look at Bernie's little black and white body and wanted to know more about her new sibling.

At first, Bernie was a little too nervous to get close to the big cat. He'd race from one hiding spot under the couch to another hiding spot under the dresser. It seemed as if Bernie *wanted* to hang out, but he was still figuring out exactly what to make of Galaxy. But the rat soon realized that Galaxy was a friend, not a foe. From then on, the main reason Bernie would race around was so he could get closer to Galaxy!

These two buddies have a pretty standard daily routine. First, Galaxy chases Bernie down the hall. Then, Bernie chases Galaxy across the rug. Then, it's Galaxy's turn again. Maybe this time Galaxy will pull Bernie in for a playful hug-wrestle-lick-cuddle. It's her classic move. When he needs a breather, Bernie dives under the couch for a quick time-out. But he's never gone for long! He'll return to lick the inside of Galaxy's ear, run across her belly, or curl up in his favorite spot—snug as a bug between his best friend's front paws.

LOLA AND PEPPER

Rabbits are born without fur.

📍 Las Vegas, Nevada

All it took was one meeting—and a sniff and a lick—for Lola and Pepper to become best friends. This noisy odd couple spends each day playing games. Making a racket on the stairs is one of their favorites. Lola is a runner, and Pepper is a hopper. Together, they zoom down the stairs of their house!

After a stair race, it's time to play hide-and-seek. The game starts when Pepper uses her great burrowing skills to hide away under a cozy blanket. It's up to Lola to use her excellent sense of smell to find her long-eared friend.

Once Pepper roots out Lola's hiding spot, they both want to play some more. Lola will run around her bunny friend, tail wagging, body bouncing and zooming. She wants to play chase! But Pepper is happy to just watch her friend dance.

The dog and the bunny's energetic friendship was put to the test when Lola got sick. When that happened, Lola couldn't play with Pepper like she was used to. She couldn't run up and down the stairs or even find Pepper burrowed in the blankets. The dog just hid behind some pillows and whimpered. But Pepper knew just what to do to help her friend. She hopped over to Lola and used her tiny bunny nose to nuzzle Lola's face. Pepper nuzzled Lola's nose, her eyes, and her ears. Soon, Lola stopped whimpering and fell asleep. Pepper is such a good nurse to Lola. Sometimes friendship is the best medicine!

Cavalier King Charles spaniels are named for King Charles II, king of England, Scotland, and Ireland in the 1600s.

SPARROW AND BERTY

There's nothing better than snuggling with your best friend! That's especially true for Sparrow and Berty. Sometimes they cuddle back-to-back. Other times it's head against tummy. But usually, these two friends cuddle like a bowl of furry spaghetti: arms, legs, tails, and heads all mixed together. These friends both had pretty rough lives at first, but now they're the perfect happy pair!

Sparrow was abandoned as a puppy, but luckily he found his forever home. Despite everything he's gone through, Sparrow is calm and patient. That makes him the perfect role model for the puppies at his doggy day care. Whenever Sparrow goes to day care, he teaches the other dogs how to have good manners just like him!

> National Pit Bull Awareness Day happens at the end of October.

His buddy, Berty the cat, needed to learn manners, too. Berty was a feral kitten. That means she was totally wild and not ready to be around people. Her human mom rescued her one year on the Fourth of July. That's why her name is Liberty, or Berty for short. Berty loves to sit in the sunny window of her apartment to keep a watchful eye on everything down below.

But her favorite thing to do is hang out with her brother, Sparrow. The cat likes to place one paw on Sparrow's head before she gives him his daily bath. Berty licks one of Sparrow's eyes, and then Sparrow uses his giant tongue to clean Berty's entire head—*slurp!* After that, it's back to cuddling!

Tortoiseshell cats like Berty are almost always female.

GEORGE

AND DEBBIE

📍 Ohio, USA

George joined Lindsay's family when he was just a nine-month-old pup. Even then, this giant dog already weighed close to seventy pounds. That's a lot of dog! He was in bad shape when he was rescued. Lindsay wasn't sure how the scared puppy would react to his new home and the foster animals who lived there. Luckily, George gets along great with everyone—animals and humans! In fact, George is so gentle with every animal he meets that his family calls him Nana George.

George is a Bordeaux mastiff, a French breed known for their wrinkly faces and major drool!

Right away, George started to mother Lindsay's baby foster animals: cleaning them, cuddling them, and making sure they were safe. George has helped his family foster lots of kittens, puppies, and even chicks and ducklings. But George had the closest bond with a tiny piglet named Debbie.

Debbie was the runt of her litter. She was just three weeks old when Lindsay's family rescued her. As soon as George met Debbie, he took on his role of Nana. At first, these two friends spent a lot of their time taking long naps and giving each other kisses and cuddles. Now that Debbie's older (and bigger!), they mostly play. George and Debbie make a lot of noise racing around the house, barking and snorting.

George has shown Debbie so much love that the pig has followed in his footsteps. She acts like Nana Debbie to the foster animals, kissing and cuddling all the cats and ducks she can find. What a loving family!

Pigs don't have great eyesight, but they make up for it with an excellent sense of smell.

PUPPI AND BURMA

📍 Southern Oregon

Some therapy dogs visit schools and libraries to read books with children.

There are three members of the Adventure Therapy Pack: Stephen (a human), Puppi (a dog), and Burma (a cat). Together, these three friends spend their days exploring the Oregon wilderness. Before the three of them found each other, they each lived alone. Now they are never apart.

Stephen found Puppi stranded on the top of a mountain. Puppi didn't seem to have anyone to take care of him, so Stephen brought him home. They met Burma several years later. She lived on the streets all by herself, so Stephen brought her home, too.

Stephen had been a soldier in the Iraq War. Once he returned home from combat, he found it stressful to be in some everyday situations. So Puppi and Burma became Stephen's therapy animals. Taking a long hike with Puppi and Burma helps Stephen stay calm. Stephen calls it Adventure Therapy.

All three members of the pack love to hike. At first, Stephen wasn't sure if a cat could keep up with an energetic dog like Puppi. But it turned out that Burma was full of energy, too. Once they are out in the open, all three enjoy swimming through streams, sprinting along forest trails, and scrambling up mountains. At the end of the day, they all stop to enjoy the sunset. Burma might tease Puppi by pawing at his tail. Puppi might sniff Burma with his snout. Whatever happens, this odd couple is just happy they get to spend their days together.

Therapy cats like Burma need to be calm, friendly, and okay with new situations.

MISSY

AND

SMUDGE

Favorite trick: opening a closed door.

📍 Harrisonburg, Virginia

Rabbits in the wild might rapidly drum their hind legs to warn other rabbits about something dangerous—*thump, thump, thump!* However, in one woman's *not*-wild home, a little rabbit named Missy thumps for a different reason. That's the sound Missy makes when she wants to get her cat brother's attention! Rabbits aren't as vocal as other animals. Instead, they use their powerful back legs to communicate.

Favorite snack: blueberries.

Missy is a Holland lop bunny. Like all lops, her ears hang downward instead of standing straight up. Missy loves snacking on blueberries, shredding a nice big sheet of tissue paper, and playing with her best bud, Smudge.

Smudge is a velvety black cat with a white tummy and white toes. In the wild, cats often chase rabbits and pounce on them for food. In their home, Smudge will certainly chase Missy and even pounce in her direction, but he would never to try to eat his best friend! Although Smudge can be moody with his human, Tara, he is nothing but gentle with Missy. In fact, in their friendship, Missy is the sassy, spunky one!

When Missy and Smudge are not chasing each other around or snuggling on the couch, this odd couple loves to take walks in the garden together. When they step out they always look sharp: Smudge in a bright blue harness and Missy in bright red. If Smudge lags behind, Missy will ask him to hurry up and join her. How? With a *thump, thump, thump*!

CHOWDER AND THE CREW

Southern California

Chowder had a rough start to life. His first family didn't expect the tiny little piglet to get so big. They couldn't care for him properly. They left Chowder outside, all alone, until they could find him a new home.

Chowder was eventually rescued by a woman named Shelby. His new family included five rescue dogs: Rika, Slick, Nya, James, and Bashe. This big group was made up of pups of all different breeds, colors, and sizes. Even though they had probably never met a pig before, the dogs soon learned to love their new sibling, just as they had learned to love each other.

Pigs and dogs have a lot in common. They are both smart and understand human instructions, they will roll over and let you rub their tummies, and they can play catch. And when it comes to Chowder and the crew, both pig and dogs will line up to get a spoonful of peanut butter every morning.

However, Chowder thinks he's too mature to actually *play* with his doggy siblings. While the dogs race around the yard, Chowder sits calmly in his wading pool. While the pups leap and bound over each other, Chowder snacks on the popcorn that falls out of his favorite treat-stuffed toy.

If Chowder were a human, he'd probably roll his eyes at the goofy crew of dogs. But Shelby can tell that Chowder loves his canine brothers and sisters. He likes when his dogs are close—just not too close!

Dogs are social animals who often prefer to live in packs.

Vietnamese potbellied pigs can weigh up to 200 pounds.

MAEVE
AND RAYLAN

📍 Canada

Raylan is a smart dog who knows how to do lots of really helpful things. Raylan's owner trained him to bring her a drink from the fridge, use a light switch, and even carry a bouquet of flowers. But there's one thing she never had to train Raylan to do: be a cat dad.

Raylan has helped his owner foster dozens of tiny kittens. When his human brings them home—usually from the same animal shelter where she adopted Raylan—the kittens can be shy and timid. But after spending some time with

When a dog leans against you, that's their version of a hug—just without using arms!

Raylan, the kittens are happy, playful, and ready to join their forever families.

Most of Raylan's friendships begin with a pile of furry animals napping in a heap. Raylan is happiest if he has a kitten by his tail, another snuggled in his armpit, and a few more around his belly. The dog has had special relationships with lots of kittens, but one really captured his heart. That was Maeve, an itty-bitty kitten with black fur and amber eyes.

This big dog and little kitten love to spend time together. First, Maeve will curl up with Raylan for a snooze or maybe a bath from Raylan's big tongue. After that, it's time for wrestling. That's when Raylan wrinkles up his nose and lets out a fake growl. Then Maeve will swat his snout. Raylan's always sure to be super careful with the little kittens during playtime. He knows that sometimes the best friends come in the tiniest packages!

A female cat can be called a molly or a queen, and a male cat can be called a tom.

CHARLOTTE AND WALLACE

Wallace is an occasionally grumpy—but always adorable—guinea pig. This breed is called a skinny pig. Skinny pigs have hair on their muzzles, feet, and legs, but they're hairless everywhere else. This makes them look thinner than most guinea pigs, but they're actually about the same size. Wallace's human mom, Aibrielle, makes him cozy sweaters from fuzzy socks to help him stay warm.

For a long time, Wallace didn't have any friends. Other guinea pigs made him nervous. Humans made him nervous. Pretty much everything made Wallace nervous! Wallace would shriek or chatter his teeth to tell people to leave him alone. But now Wallace "popcorns" by jumping straight up in the air. This is Aibrielle's favorite thing to see, because it means Wallace is very happy. Wallace usually does this when he is around his best friend, Charlotte.

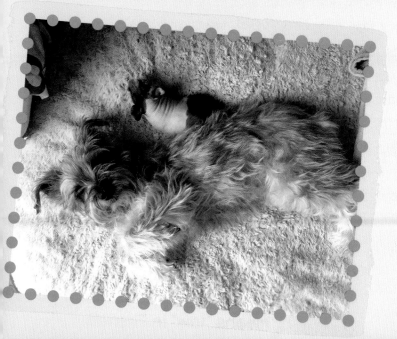

Charlotte is a silly, cheerful terrier. She used to be a service dog for kids. Charlotte doesn't really like to be around other dogs. But she loves to be around her brother, Wallace. As soon as she wakes up, Charlotte heads over to Wallace's crate and gives him a good sniff. Then it's time to play! Charlotte likes to get down close to the ground so she and Wallace can see eye to eye. From there she'll prance and jump around in her own version of a happy guinea pig popcorn. And at the end of the day, this odd couple is always happy to snuggle up together for a snooze.

BUTTERBALL, NELLIE, AND DIXIE

Atlanta, Georgia

Butterball has soft white feathers, a smooth orange bill, and orange webbed feet. When her human mom, Katherine, talks to her, Butterball quacks back. Butterball is a duck, but she doesn't seem to know that! She thinks she's a dog, just like her best friends Nellie and Dixie.

Butterball loves to do everything with her basset hound sisters. For instance, when Nellie and Dixie head outside for their daily walk, Butterball waddles right behind them. The first time this happened, Katherine figured Butterball would turn around after a few yards. But Butterball trotted along behind the dogs, swaying back and forth in her ducky way, for their whole walk.

Nellie and Dixie are easygoing dogs, so they don't mind Butterball hanging around. Like most basset hounds, they enjoy the company of other animals—

"Basset hound" comes from the word "bas," which means "low" in French.

96

Groups of ducks walk in a line to keep an eye out for predators.

even the quacking kind! (Plus, Dixie likes to nap in Butterball's nest of hay!) Once they get back home after a walk, it's usually time for dinner. And when Katherine puts kibble out for Nellie and Dixie, Butterball rushes over for a bite, too!

If Nellie and Dixie are busy, Butterball happily spends her time with some of the other rescue animals in the family. She loves exploring with Hollywood the cat, snuggling with the rabbits, and visiting with the chickens. All of the animals in the house get along. And they especially love to hang out together in Katherine's art studio and watch her paint. It doesn't hurt that she's usually painting a picture of her animals!

SIMBA

AND HENRY

📍 Nebo, North Carolina

C andy doesn't need an alarm clock: a giant bunny wakes her up instead! His name is Henry, and he's a two-and-a-half-foot long, 20-pound Flemish giant rabbit. Every morning he jumps onto his mom's bed to remind her that it's time for breakfast: rolled oats, grapes, and apples. Yum! Just what a bunny needs before heading off to work.

Henry is a therapy rabbit. A few times a month, he and Candy head to a nearby hospital or senior center to visit with the patients there. The patients are always happy to see this Flemish giant. He's like a big, fuzzy stuffed animal—perfect for hugs!

When he's not doing this very important work, Henry gets to spend the rest of his time with his cat brother. Simba's a white cat with light brown points on his ears

Colorpoint kittens are born white and develop their points a week or two after birth.

and tail. You can usually find Simba lounging near his bunny friend while Henry munches on hay. Otherwise, he's off looking for a gift to bring back for his friend. But it's not usually a very good gift. Once he brought Henry a four-foot-long live snake—yikes!

These two best friends love to spend some time each day exploring the garden. If they're lucky, they might spot a few deer to make friends with. Then Simba plops down on a flat rock while Henry has another grassy snack. It's always a great way to end the day!

Flemish giants are one of the largest breeds of rabbit—one record-breaker grew more than four feet long!

ELLA
AND
WILLOW

Every cat's nose has a unique print—just like a human fingerprint.

📍 Florida

Willow the cat is pretty special. She was born with a chromosomal defect that kept her nose from developing in the typical way.

Willow knew she would need a home, so she found one all by herself. A woman named Lori found the little kitten on her doorstep. Lori was worried that Willow wouldn't be able to find a home at a shelter because she looked different from the other cats. So she decided the kitten's new home would be with her!

Lori rescued Willow at exactly the right time. Her boxer, Ella, needed a playmate. Ella is a sweet, silly, smart dog. And, like most boxers, Ella is also big and strong and has a lot of energy. Before Willow came along, Ella was so playful that she could be a little too intense. When she's around her new kitten sister, Ella becomes much calmer. She's always gentle with Willow—until it's time to box, that is!

These two animal besties are always wrestling and play-fighting. Willow usually starts the boxing session. First, she gives a few paw taps to the side of Ella's nose. Ella will duck and weave. Sometimes she gives the kitty a playful nip back with a pretend fierce—but mostly sweet—face.

The sisters also love playing with bouncy pipe cleaners. They are the only toy Willow likes! And, of course, no day would be complete without a quick grooming session, ending with a cuddly nap.

Boxers didn't become a popular dog breed in the United States until the 1930s.

WHICH STORY SHOULD YOU READ?

DO YOU WANT TO READ ABOUT A DOG?
Try checking out these stories:

DO YOU WANT TO READ ABOUT A CAT?
Try checking out these stories:

Dogs and cats are BFFs in 14 of these stories.

There are 10 golden retrievers in these stories!

Henry is a Flemish giant, and he's more than 2 feet long!

Quack! All but one of these bird stories are about ducks.

There are 7 stories about pigs!

The rodents in these stories are guinea pigs, rats, and squirrels.

Lions and tigers and monkeys—oh my!

For more real animal stories, check out

dodo kids